MORE FREE STUFF FOR KIDS

Our Pledge

We have collected and examined the best free and up-to-a-dollar offers that we could find (plus a few extra-special over-a-dollar values!). Each supplier in this book has promised to honor properly made requests for **single items** through **1994**. Though mistakes do happen, we will do our best to make sure this book really works.

Meadowbrook Press

Distributed by Simon & Schuster
New York

The Free Stuff Editors

Director: Bruce Lansky
Editor/Researcher: Cathy Broberg
Managing Editor: Elizabeth H. Weiss
Production Manager: Kate Laing
Desktop Publishing Coordinator: Jon C. Wright
Keyliner: Erik Broberg

ISBN: 0-88166-204-6
Simon & Schuster Ordering #: 0-671-88082-9

ISSN: 1065-5093
Second Edition

Published by Meadowbrook Press, 18318 Minnetonka Boulevard, Deephaven, MN 55391.

BOOK TRADE DISTRIBUTION by Simon & Schuster, a division of Simon and Schuster, Inc., 1230 Avenue of the Americas, New York, NY 10020.

93 94   5 4 3 2 1

Printed in the United States of America

Contents

Thank You's iv

Using This Book 1

More Free Stuff for Kids Checklist 8

SPORTS
Basketball 10
Sports Collectibles 14
Recreation 16
Fitness 20

STICKERS
Yummy Stickers 22
Activity Stickers 23
Novelty Stickers 24
Holiday Stickers 25
Creature Stickers 26

HOLIDAYS
Valentine's Day 28
Easter 29
Mother's & Father's Days 30
Independence Day 31
Halloween 32
Chanukah 34
Christmas 35
Birthdays 36

SAVE THE ANIMALS
Wildlife 38
Marine Life 41
Saving Animals 42
Animal Info 44
Ethics 46

COLLECTIONS AND HOBBIES
Coin Collections 48
Stamp Collections 49
General Collections 50
Models 53
Music 54
Games 55

Magic 56
Catalogs 57
Amusements 58

MATH, SCIENCE, AND COMPUTERS
Math 60
Economics 61
Industry 62
Science 63
Computers 66

WRITING SUPPLIES
Pencils 68
Writing Materials 70
Erasers 71
Pens 72
Postcards 73
Stationery 74

WORLD CULTURES
Native Americans 76
African Americans 77
Cultural Diversity 78
Other Countries 79
World Peoples 84

AWARENESS AND SELF-ESTEEM
Disabilities 86
Drug Awareness 88
Safety 89
Growing Up 90
Self-Esteem 92

JEWELRY AND CRAFTS
Necklaces 94
Bracelets 96
Pins and Buttons 98
Art Materials 99
Crafts 101

Index 103

Thank You's

To Pat Blakely, Barbara Haislet, and Judith Hentges for creating and publishing the original *Rainbow Book,* and for proving that kids, parents, and teachers would respond enthusiastically to a source of free things by mail. They taught us the importance of carefully checking the quality of each item and doing our best to make sure that each and every request is satisfied.

Our heartfelt appreciation goes to hundreds of organizations and individuals for making this book possible. The suppliers and editors of this book have a common goal: to make it possible for kids to reach out and discover the world by themselves.

MEADOWBROOK PRESS
1994 EDITION

U.S. MAIL

USING THIS BOOK

About This Book

More Free Stuff for Kids contains listings of hundreds of items to send away for. The Free Stuff Editors have examined every item and think they're among the best offers available. There are no trick offers—only safe, fun, and informative things you'll like!

This book is designed for kids who can read and write. The directions in **Using This Book** explain exactly how to request an item. Read the instructions carefully so you know how to send a request. Making sure you've filled out a request correctly is easy—just complete the *More Free Stuff for Kids* **Checklist** on p. 8. Half the fun is using the book on your own. The other half is getting a real reward for your efforts!

Each year the Free Stuff Editors create a new edition of this book, taking out old items, inserting new ones, and changing addresses and prices. It is important for you to use an updated edition because the suppliers only honor properly made requests for single items in the **current** edition. If you use this edition after **1994,** your request might not be honored.

Getting Your Book in Shape

Before sending for free stuff, get your book in shape. Fold it open one page at a time, working from the two ends toward the middle. This will make the book lie flat when you read or copy addresses.

Reading Carefully

Read the descriptions of the offers carefully to find out exactly what you're getting. Here are some guidelines to help you know what you're sending for:

• A pamphlet or foldout is usually one sheet of paper folded over and printed on both sides.

• A booklet is usually larger and contains more pages, but it's smaller than a book.

Following Directions

It's important to follow each supplier's directions. On one offer, you might need to use a postcard. On another offer, you might be asked to include money or a long self-addressed, stamped envelope. If you do not follow the directions **exactly,** you might not get your request. Ask for only **one** of anything you send for. Family or classroom members using the same book must send separate requests.

Sending Postcards

A postcard is a small card you can write on and send through the mail without an envelope. Many suppliers offering free items require you to send requests on postcards. Please do this. It saves them the time it takes to open many envelopes.

The post office sells postcards with pre-printed postage. The cost of these postcards is 19¢. You can also buy postcards at a drugstore and put stamps on them yourself. (Postcards with a picture on them are usually more expensive.) You must use a postcard that is at least 3 ½ by 5 ½ inches. (The post office will not take 3-by-5-inch index cards.) Your postcards should be addressed like the one below.

Jessie Rogers
2415 Lake Street
Solon Springs, WI 54873

USA 19

The Nature Conservancy
Member Relations
1815 North Lynn Street
Arlington, VA 22209

Dear Sir or Madam:

Please send me a coloring poster.

Thank you very much.

Sincerely,
Jessie Rogers

2415 Lake Street
Solon Springs, WI 54873

- **Neatly print** the supplier's address on the side of the postcard that has the postage. Put your return address in the upper left-hand corner of that side as well.

- **Neatly print** your request, your name, and your address on the blank side of the postcard.

- Do not abbreviate the name of your street or city.

- Use a ballpoint pen.

Sending Letters

Your letters should look like the one below.

- **Neatly print** the name of the item you want exactly as you see it in the directions.
- **Neatly print** your own name and address at the bottom of the letter. (Do not abbreviate the name of your street or city.)
- If you're including coins or a long self-addressed, stamped envelope, say so in the letter.
- Put a first-class stamp (they cost 29¢) on any envelope you send. You can get stamps at the post office.
- **Neatly print** the supplier's address in the center of the envelope and your return address in the upper left-hand corner.
- If you're sending many letters at once, make sure you put the right letter in the right envelope.
- Use a ballpoint pen. Pencil can be difficult to read, and ink pen often smears.

Sending a Long Self-Addressed, Stamped Envelope

If the directions say to enclose a long self-addressed, stamped envelope, here's how to do it:

- **Neatly print** your name and address in the center of a 9½-inch long envelope as if you were mailing it to yourself. Print your return address in the upper left-hand corner of the envelope as well. Put a first-class stamp on it.
- Fold up (but don't seal!) the long self-addressed, stamped envelope, and put it inside another 9½-inch long envelope (along with your letter to the supplier) and put a first-class stamp on it.
- **Neatly print** the supplier's address in the center of the envelope you are sending and your **return** address in the upper left-hand corner.
- Use a ballpoint pen.

Jessie Rogers
2415 Lake Street
Solon Springs, WI 54873

Jessie Rogers
2415 Lake Street
Solon Springs, WI 54873

Sending Money

Many of the suppliers in this book are not charging you for their items. However, the cost of postage and handling is high today, and suppliers must charge you for this. If the directions say to enclose money for postage and handling, you must do so. Here are a few rules about sending money:

- Tape the coins to your letter so they won't break out of the envelope.
- Don't stack your coins on top of each other in the envelope.
- If an item costs $1.00, send a one-dollar bill instead of coins. Don't tape dollar bills.
- Send only U.S. money.
- If a grown-up is helping you, he/she may write a check (unless the directions say otherwise).
- Send all money directly to the suppliers—their addresses are listed with their offers.

Sending a Mailing Label

Some suppliers might ask you to send a mailing label with your address on it. Please do this. It makes it easier for them to process your order. Some offers on pages 26, 55, and 66 require a mailing label!

You can buy mailing labels at the drugstore. When sending a mailing label to a supplier, **neatly print** or type your address on it. Leave the sticky backing on the label and put it in the envelope.

```
Jessie Rogers
2415 Lake Street
Solon Springs, WI 54873
```

Getting Your Free Stuff

Expect to wait four to eight weeks for your free stuff to arrive. Sometimes you have to wait longer. Remember, suppliers get thousands of requests each year. Please be patient!

Making Sure You Get Your Request

The Free Stuff Editors have tried to make the directions for using this book as clear as possible to make sure you get what you send for. But you must follow **all** of the directions **exactly** as they're written, or the supplier will not be able to answer your request. If you're confused about the directions, ask a grown-up to help you.

Do's and Don'ts:

- **Do** use a ballpoint pen.
- **Do** print. Cursive can be difficult to read.
- **Do** print your name, address, and zip code clearly and fully on the postcard or on the envelope **and** the letter you send. Do not abbreviate anything except state names. Abbreviations can be confusing, and sometimes envelopes and letters get separated after they reach the supplier.
- **Do** send the correct amount of U.S. money, but use as few coins as possible.

- **Do** tape the coins you send to the letter you send them with. If you don't, the money might rip the envelope and fall out.
- **Do** use a 9½-inch long self-addressed, stamped envelope if the instructions say you should.
- **Do not** ask for more than **one** of an item.
- **Do not** stack coins in the envelope.
- **Do not** seal your long self-addressed, stamped envelope. The suppliers need to put the item you ordered in the envelope you send.
- **Do not** ask Meadowbrook Press to send you any of the items listed in the book unless you are ordering the Meadowbrook offers from p. 30 or p. 57. The publishers of this book do not carry items belonging to other suppliers. They do not supply refunds, either.

Follow all the rules to avoid disappointment!

What to Do If You Aren't Satisfied:

If you have complaints about any offer, or if you don't receive the items you sent for within eight to ten weeks, contact the Free Stuff Editors. Before you complain, please reread the directions. Are you sure you followed them properly? Are you using this **1994** edition **after** 1994? (Offers here are only good for 1993 and 1994.) The Free Stuff Editors won't be able to send you the item, but they can make sure that any suppliers who don't fulfill requests are dropped from next year's *More Free Stuff for Kids*. We'd like to know which offers you like and what kind of new offers you'd like us to add to next year's edition. So don't be bashful—write us a letter. Send your complaints or suggestions to:

The Free Stuff Editors
Meadowbrook Press
18318 Minnetonka Boulevard
Deephaven, MN 55391

More Free Stuff for Kids Checklist

Use this checklist each time you send out a request. It will help you follow directions exactly and prevent mistakes. Put a check mark in the box each time you complete a task—you can photocopy this page and use it again and again.

When sending postcards and letters:

❏ I used a ballpoint pen.

❏ I printed neatly and carefully.

❏ I asked for the correct item (only one).

❏ I wrote to the correct supplier.

❏ I double-checked the supplier's address.

When sending postcards only:

❏ I put my return address on the postcard.

❏ I applied a 19¢ stamp (if the postage wasn't pre-printed).

When sending letters only:

❏ I put my return address on the letter.

❏ I included a long self-addressed, stamped envelope (if the directions asked for one).

❏ I included the correct amount of money (if the directions asked for money).

❏ I put my return address on the envelope.

❏ I applied a 29¢ stamp.

When sending a long self-addressed, stamped envelope:

❏ I used a 9½-inch long envelope.

❏ I put my address on the front of the envelope.

❏ I put my return address in the upper left-hand corner of the envelope.

❏ I left the envelope unsealed.

❏ I applied a 29¢ stamp.

When sending a one-dollar bill:

❏ I sent U.S. money.

❏ I enclosed a one-dollar bill with my letter instead of coins.

When sending coins:

❏ I sent U.S. money.

❏ I taped the coins to my letter.

❏ I did not stack the coins on top of each other.

When sending a mailing label:

❏ I printed or typed my address.

❏ I left the sticky backing on the label.

❏ I put the label in the envelope.

MEADOWBROOK PRESS
1994
EDITION

U.S.
MAIL

SPORTS

BASKETBALL

The Hawks

Help the Atlanta Hawks soar next year! Send for this Eastern Conference NBA team's bumper sticker to show your support.

Directions:	Write your request on paper, and put it in an envelope. You must enclose a long self-addressed, stamped envelope.
Write to:	Atlanta Hawks PR Department One CNN Center, Suite 405 Atlanta, GA 30303 Attention: Fan Mail
Ask for:	Hawks bumper sticker

The Clippers

See how they play in L.A.! Los Angeles is a great basketball town with two pro teams calling it home. The L.A. Clippers will send you a sticker, schedule, and team brochure (depending on availability) so that you can root for them.

Directions:	Write your request on paper, and put it in an envelope. You must enclose a long self-addressed, stamped envelope.
Write to:	Los Angeles Clippers Los Angeles Sports Arena 3939 South Figueroa Street Los Angeles, CA 90037-1292 Attention: Fan Mail
Ask for:	Clippers fan pack

BASKETBALL

The Pistons

The shot is up…and SWISH! The Detroit Pistons are one of the NBA's most successful teams. Send for their fan pack that includes a team schedule and an 8½-by-11-inch team photo (depending on availability).

Directions:	Use a postcard.
Write to:	Detroit Pistons Two Championship Drive Auburn Hills, MI 48326 Attention: Fan Mail
Ask for:	Pistons fan pack

The 76ers

Slam dunk! One of the eight original NBA teams has an offer you'll want to jump at. Send for this Philadelphia 76ers bumper sticker to show your support.

BASKETBALL AT THE SPEED OF SIGHT

Directions:	Write your request on paper, and put it in an envelope. You must enclose a long self-addressed, stamped envelope.
Write to:	Philadelphia 76ers Basketball Public Relations at Executive Offices Veterans Stadium P.O. Box 25040 Philadelphia, PA 19148
Ask for:	76ers bumper sticker

Hall of Fame

Where can you see an actual pair of bronzed size 22 sneakers? At the Basketball Hall of Fame! Read all about this "fan-tastic" museum that really makes basketball come alive.

Directions:	Write your request on paper, and put it in an envelope. You must enclose a long self-addressed, stamped envelope.
Write to:	Basketball Hall of Fame 1150 West Columbus Avenue Springfield, MA 01105
Ask for:	HOF pamphlet

Basketball's History

Back in 1891, a physical education professor wanted to help his students chase away the winter blues and ended up creating America's most popular indoor sport—basketball! This 35-page booklet covers the rules of the game, its origin, history, and more.

Directions:	Write your request on paper, and put it in an envelope. You must enclose a long self-addressed, stamped envelope and **$1.00**.
Write to:	Basketball Hall of Fame 1150 West Columbus Avenue Springfield, MA 01105
Ask for:	Basketball Was Born Here booklet

Pencil-Top Hoops

Take a fast break from your homework with this pencil-top basketball game. Just slip the mini hoop and backboard onto your pencil, and give yourself two points every time you get the string-attached ball into the hoop.

Directions:	Write your request on paper, and put it in an envelope. You must enclose a long self-addressed, stamped envelope and **75¢** for **one** game or a long self-addressed, stamped envelope and **$1.00** for **two**.
Write to:	Marlene Monroe Department BT 6210 Ridge Manor Drive Memphis, TN 38115-3411
Ask for:	Pencil-top hoop(s)

Football Cards

Hey, NFL fans! If you collect football cards, you'll love this offer. You'll get sixteen different football cards with NFL stars and stats.

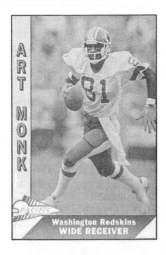

Directions:	Write your request on paper, and put it in an envelope. You must enclose a long self-addressed, stamped envelope and **75¢**.
Write to:	DANORS Department F 5721 Funston Street, Bay 14 Hollywood, FL 33023
Ask for:	Sixteen football cards

Basketball Cards

Take a halftime break to learn more about your favorite NBA players with these fourteen basketball cards. Add the cards in this pack to your collection or trade them with your friends.

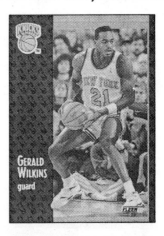

Directions:	Write your request on paper, and put it in an envelope. You must enclose a long self-addressed, stamped envelope and **75¢**.
Write to:	DANORS Department B 5721 Funston Street, Bay 14 Hollywood, FL 33023
Ask for:	Fourteen basketball cards

Bendable Athletes

These bendable sports figures are fun to collect and display. You can make them sit, bend over, or stand on their head. There's a basketball, football, baseball, soccer, and tennis player. You'll get two.

Directions:	Write your request on paper, and put it in an envelope. You must enclose **$1.00** and **one 29¢** stamp. (*No checks please.*)
Write to:	Safe Child P.O. Box 40 1594 Brooklyn, NY 11240-1594
Ask for:	Two bendable sports figures (*The supplier reserves the right to choose which figures you'll get.*)

Sports Stickers

Be a sport! These sticker sheets feature baseballs, soccer balls, bowling pins, and more! You'll get two sheets.

Directions:	Write your request on paper, and put it in an envelope. You must enclose a long self-addressed, stamped envelope and **$1.00.**
Write to:	Marlene Monroe Department SS 6210 Ridge Manor Drive Memphis, TN 38115
Ask for:	Sports stickers

Footbag (Hacky Sack®)

Footbag is fun! Learn all about this fun sport with this issue of *Footbag World* magazine and a players' manual. You'll even get a lifetime membership card for the World Footbag Association.

Directions: Write your request on paper (*include your address, phone number with area code, and date of birth*), and put it in an envelope. You must enclose **$1.00**.

Write to: World Footbag Association
1317 Washington Avenue, Suite 7
Golden, CO 80401

Ask for: Kids' membership

Boomerang

Boomerangs were originally invented thousands of years ago as a Stone-Age tool. Today, boomerangs are used for recreation. Send for this pattern and instruction sheet to learn how to make your own boomerang out of household materials.

Directions: Write your request on paper, and put it in an envelope. You must enclose a long self-addressed, stamped envelope and **25¢**.

Write to: U.S. Boomerang Association
P.O. Box 182
Delaware, OH 43015

Ask for: "More Free Stuff for Kids" packet

Pool

Did you know that "pool is cool" with stars like Tom Cruise, Madonna, and Eddie Murphy? No matter what your age or ability, you can be a "hot shot" by playing pool! Find out more in this illustrated booklet that shows you all the right moves and the rules of 8-ball.

Directions:	Write your request on paper, and put it in an envelope. You must enclose a long self-addressed, stamped envelope with **two 29¢** stamps.
Write to:	Billiard Congress of America 1700 South 1st Avenue Eastdale Plaza Iowa City, IA 52240
Ask for:	How to Play Pool Right booklet

Canoeing

Can you canoe? The answer is yes if you learn how to get the canoe in the water, paddle, and stay safe as you move through the water. This pamphlet is full of tips and safety reminders.

Directions:	Write your request on paper, and put it in an envelope. You must enclose a long self-addressed, stamped envelope.
Write to:	United States Canoe Association 606 Ross Street Middletown, OH 45044-5062 Attention: Jim Mack
Ask for:	Welcome Paddler! pamphlet

Horseshoes

Horseshoes aren't just for horses or good luck! Throw a ringer at your next family picnic by taking along this instructional pamphlet that explains the rules and scoring.

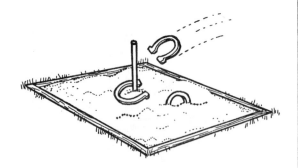

Directions:	Use a postcard.
Write to:	NHPA RR #2, Box 178 La Monte, MO 65337
Ask for:	Rules of Horseshoe Pitching pamphlet

Archery

If you've ever wished you could shoot an arrow like Robin Hood, here's your chance. Take up the sport of archery and learn to master a bow and arrow. This illustrated booklet will help you get started.

Directions:	Use a postcard.
Write to:	Ben Pearson Archery Customer Service P.O. Box 11805 Fort Smith, AR 72917-1805
Ask for:	ABC's of Archery booklet

Hiking Safety

Do you like adventures? Hiking is a great way to explore nature, exercise, and have lots of fun. This pamphlet is full of tips and safety reminders.

Directions:	Use a postcard.
Write to:	American Hiking Society P.O. Box 20160 Washington, DC 22041-2160
Ask for:	Hiking Safety pamphlet

Yo-Yo Tricks

This fun and informative trick sheet will show you yo-yo tricks like "The Creeper," "Walk the Dog," and "Loop the Loop." You'll be a whiz with a yo-yo in no time.

Directions:	Write your request on paper, and put it in an envelope. You must enclose a long self-addressed, stamped envelope.
Write to:	Duncan Toys Department MFSFK P.O. Box 5 Middlefield, OH 44062
Ask for:	Duncan trick sheet

Exercise

Do you want to get physically fit? This illustrated booklet will help you meet the President's fitness challenge by teaching you about stretching, exercise, and motivation.

Tape Measure

It's important to set goals when you're getting in shape. This 60-inch tape measure with exercises and motivational tips will help you keep a record of your progress as you inch your way to better health.

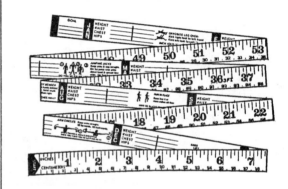

Directions:	Use a postcard.
Write to:	The President's Challenge Poplars Research Center 400 East Seventh Street Bloomington, IN 47405
Ask for:	Get Fit! booklet

Directions:	Write your request on paper, and put it in an envelope. You must enclose **75¢.**
Write to:	Special Products Department MF 34 Romeyn Avenue Amsterdam, NY 12010
Ask for:	Fitness tape measure

MEADOWBROOK PRESS
1994
EDITION

U.S.
MAIL

STICKERS

Blueberry Stickers

These stickers look good enough to eat! They feature tasty blueberries in a beautiful shade of blue. You can request up to five stickers.

Soda Pop Stickers

These stickers look and smell great! One sticker sheet features a cool drink that smells like cola. The other features root beer floats that smell simply delicious. Each sheet has twelve big stickers.

Directions:	Write your request on paper, and put it in an envelope. You must enclose a long self-addressed, stamped envelope.
Write to:	Blueberry Council Department MFSFK P.O. Box 166 Marmora, NJ 08223
Ask for:	Blueberry stickers (*Specify the amount you want.*)

Directions:	Write your request on paper, and put it in an envelope. You must enclose **$1.00** for **each** sheet you request.
Write to:	The Very Best Sticker Company Department MC-94 P.O. Box 2838 Long Beach, CA 90801-2838
Ask for:	• Cool Stuff sticker sheet • Great Stuff sticker sheet

Scene Stickers

These activity sticker sheets will keep you busy and make your sticker book look really creative. Each one has lots of brightly colored stickers for designing your own fun scene. The supplier will send you two different scenes—it's a surprise which ones you'll get!

Directions: Write your request on paper, and put it in an envelope. You must enclose **$1.00.**

Write to: Smiles 'n Things
P.O. Box 974
Claremont, CA 91711-0974

Ask for: Activity sticker sheets

Slogan Stickers

Do you like baseball, basketball, football, soccer, tennis, golf, surfing, fishing, scuba diving, photography, computers, skateboarding, aerobics, bowling, biking, or sports in general? If you do, let people know! These big stickers feature a cartoon peanut who'll let everyone know which activities you're "nuts" about. You'll get two.

Directions:	Write your request on paper, and put it in an envelope. You must enclose a long self-addressed, stamped envelope and **$1.00**.
Write to:	LUVNUTS Stickers Sports 'n' Novelty Department 2106 Hoffnagle Street Philadelphia, PA 19152
Ask for:	LUVNUT stickers (*Specify two activities you want from the list above.*)

Fuzzy Stickers

These colorful stickers are soft and fuzzy. There are lots of pets like cats and dogs; farm animals like cows and lambs; wild animals like rabbits and mice; plus some other fun friends. You'll get twelve stickers.

Directions:	Write your request on paper, and put it in an envelope. You must enclose a long self-addressed, stamped envelope and **$1.00**.
Write to:	Expressions Department FZ 1668 Valtec Lane, Suite F Boulder, CO 80301
Ask for:	Fuzzy sticker sheet

Halloween Stickers

Here are some spooky scented stickers to really howl about. You'll get twelve witch stickers that smell like licorice. They're perfect for Halloween.

Directions:	Write your request on paper, and put it in an envelope. You must enclose **$1.00.**
Write to:	The Very Best Sticker Company Department MW-94 P.O. Box 2838 Long Beach, CA 90801-2838
Ask for:	Witch sticker sheet

Christmas Stickers

Here are twelve scented stickers that smell like holiday spices. You can use them to decorate Christmas cards or to give as a gift.

Directions:	Write your request on paper, and put it in an envelope. You must enclose **$1.00.**
Write to:	The Very Best Sticker Company Department MJ-94 P.O. Box 2838 Long Beach, CA 90801-2838
Ask for:	Joy sticker sheet

Monster Stickers

Give yourself the creeps! This sticker booklet is filled with 24 funny and mysterious creatures that will leave you scared "silly." You'll find a freaky fortune-teller, dancing skeleton, goofy four-armed man, and lots more.

Silly Stickers

These shiny stickers will really make you giggle. There are smiling circus clowns and goofy faces with all sorts of funny expressions. You'll get two sheets.

Directions: Write your request on paper, and put it in an envelope. You must enclose a **mailing label** with your return address on it, **$1.00,** and **one 29¢** stamp.

Write to: Dover Publications
Department MSB
31 East 2nd Street
Mineola, NY 11501

Ask for: Funny Monsters sticker booklet

Directions: Write your request on paper, and put it in an envelope. You must enclose a long self-addressed, stamped envelope and **$1.00.**

Write to: Mr. Rainbows
Department K-114
P.O. Box 387
Avalon, NJ 08202

Ask for: Circus clowns and funny faces sticker sheets

MEADOWBROOK PRESS
1994
EDITION

U.S.
MAIL

HOLIDAYS

Heart Erasers

Here's a great gift for your Valentine. Each of these colorful erasers features hearts and a special message. You'll get three.

Directions:	Write your request on paper, and put it in an envelope. You must enclose a long self-addressed, stamped envelope and **50¢.**
Write to:	Sav-On Department VE P.O. Box 1356 Gwinn, MI 49841
Ask for:	Three Valentine erasers

Heart Memo

Write a "Happy Valentine's Day" note to someone special using this heart-shaped mini memo pad. The cover has lots of little neon hearts, and the pages are pastel blue and pink.

Directions:	Write your request on paper, and put it in an envelope. You must enclose a long self-addressed, stamped envelope and **50¢.**
Write to:	Sav-On Department HP P.O. Box 1356 Gwinn, MI 49841
Ask for:	Heart memo pad

Easter Erasers

Give your best pals something extra for their Easter baskets. Send for these erasers that feature bright and cheery Easter scenes in fluorescent colors. You'll get three.

Directions:	Write your request on paper, and put it in an envelope. You must enclose a long self-addressed, stamped envelope and **50¢.**
Write to:	Sav-On Department EE P.O. Box 1356 Gwinn, MI 49841
Ask for:	Three Easter erasers

Easter Stickers

These prism sticker sheets are "egg-cellent!" One has pink Easter eggs with a "Happy Easter" message, and the other has the Easter Bunny in lots of different poses.

Directions:	Write your request on paper, and put it in an envelope. You must enclose a long self-addressed, stamped envelope and **$1.00.**
Write to:	Mr. Rainbows Department K-24 P.O. Box 387 Avalon, NJ 08202
Ask for:	Happy Easter and Easter Bunny sticker sheets

Key Chains

Are you looking for gift ideas for Mom and Dad on their special days? Then send for one of these key chains with a tape measure inside. One says "#1 Mom" and the other says "#1 Dad."

Directions:	Write your request on paper, and put it in an envelope. You must enclose **$1.00** for **each** key chain you request. (*No checks please.*)
Write to:	Safe Child P.O. Box 40 1594 Brooklyn, NY 11240-1594
Ask for:	• Mom key chain • Dad key chain

Button

Do you ever feel embarrassed when **your** parents do something goofy like "dress the family pet in a costume for Halloween?" This big 2¼-inch button, based on the humorous book *How to Embarrass Your Kids Without Even Trying*, is a great gag gift for Mom or Dad.

Directions:	Write your request on paper, and put it in an envelope. You must enclose **$1.00**.
Write to:	Meadowbrook Press Department HTE 18318 Minnetonka Boulevard Deephaven, MN 55391
Ask for:	Parents' button

Flag Stickers

Celebrate Independence Day with these puffy flag stickers. They stick to lots of different surfaces and are reusable—display them every Fourth of July! You'll get six.

Directions:	Write your request on paper, and put it in an envelope. You must enclose **$1.00.**
Write to:	Smiles 'n Things P.O. Box 974 Claremont, CA 91711-0974
Ask for:	Six flag stickers

Flag Pencil

You can take pride in America when you write with this red, white, and blue pencil that's covered with stars and stripes.

Directions:	Write your request on paper, and put it in an envelope. You must enclose **$1.00.**
Write to:	Sav-On Department FP P.O. Box 1356 Gwinn, MI 49841
Ask for:	American flag pencil

Trick-or-Treat Bag

You can't go trick-or-treating without something to carry all your candy in! Send for this colorful, roomy trick-or-treat bag to make your Halloween complete.

Directions:	Write your request on paper, and put it in an envelope. You must enclose a long self-addressed, stamped envelope and **25¢**.
Write to:	Sav-On Department T P.O. Box 1356 Gwinn, MI 49841
Ask for:	Trick-or-Treat bag

Trick-or-Treat Safety

Halloween is a fun holiday, and it can be even more fun when you trick-or-treat with safety in mind. This coloring and activity book is full of puzzles, mazes, and great safety tips.

Directions:	Write your request on paper, and put it in an envelope. You must enclose **$1.00**.
Write to:	Special Products Department MF 34 Romeyn Avenue Amsterdam, NY 12010
Ask for:	Have a Safe Halloween coloring book

Rubber Skeleton

This foot-long skeleton wiggles like crazy when you pick it up. It's colorful and creepy—hang it on your front door to greet your trick-or-treaters!

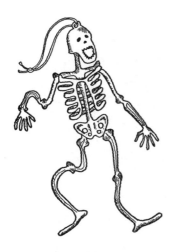

Directions:	Write your request on paper, and put it in an envelope. You must enclose **$1.00.**
Write to:	Sav-On Department RS P.O. Box 1356 Gwinn, MI 49841
Ask for:	Rubber skeleton

Scary Stencils

You can create some scary scenes with these Halloween stencils. Choose from a witch, jack-o'-lantern, skull, or "scaredy" cat—or get them all!

Directions:	Write your request on paper, and put it in an envelope. You must enclose a long self-addressed, stamped envelope for **one** or **$1.00** for **all.**
Write to:	Sav-On Department ST P.O. Box 1356 Gwinn, MI 49841
Ask for:	Scary stencil(s) (*If you're ordering only one, specify the one you want.*)

Chanukah Stickers

Celebrate the Feast of Lights with these colorful Chanukah stickers. Each little sticker sheet features a menorah surrounded by dreidels and six-pointed stars. Stick them on your notebook or share them with friends. You'll get two sheets.

Directions:	Write your request on paper, and put it in an envelope. You must enclose a long self-addressed, stamped envelope and **$1.00.**
Write to:	Mr. Rainbows Department K-104 P.O. Box 387 Avalon, NJ 08202
Ask for:	Two Chanukah sticker sheets

Homemade Ornament

Now you can have a Christmas ornament of your very own to hang on the tree. You'll get a unique homemade ornament created from a recycled Christmas card with hand-stitching all around the edges. You can even request the type of scene you might like. Be sure to order *early* so it comes in time for December!

Directions: Write your request on paper, and put it in an envelope. You must enclose a long self-addressed, stamped envelope and **$1.00.**

Write to: Beverly Scott
P.O. Box 55494
Birmingham, AL 35255-5494

Ask for: Christmas ornament

Handmade Wreath

Get in the Christmas spirit with this great mini wreath kit that includes wreath-making materials, a red ribbon, and illustrated instructions. With just a little twisting and tying, you can make a small wreath to use as a gift or to hang on your Christmas tree.

Directions: Write your request on paper, and put it in an envelope. You must enclose **$1.00.**

Write to: The Woolie Works—Wreath
6201 East Huffman Road
Anchorage, AK 99516-2440

Ask for: Wreath kit

Birthday Balloons

Give your best buddy a birthday balloon! These fun Mylar balloons feature messages like "Happy Birthday" and "I Love You" and cartoon characters like Garfield and Snoopy.

Directions: Write your request on paper, and put it in an envelope. You must enclose **$1.00** for **each** balloon you request.

Write to: Mark-It
Department 2
P.O. Box 246
Dayton, OH 45405

Ask for:
· Happy Birthday balloon
· I Love You balloon
· Garfield balloon
· Snoopy balloon

Your Birthday

Find out your birthday's place in history. This fact sheet tells you what other special events happened on your birthday. You'll learn which famous people were born, what the top songs were, and more! Specify which state you were born in to find out which famous people were born there, too.

Directions: Write your request on paper, and put it in an envelope. You must enclose a long self-addressed, stamped envelope and **$1.00**. (*Please include your birthday, age, and state you were born in.*)

Write to: Special Products
Department MF
34 Romeyn Avenue
Amsterdam, NY 12010

Ask for: Happy Birthday sheet

MEADOWBROOK PRESS

**1994
EDITION**

U.S.
MAIL

SAVE THE ANIMALS

Otters

The Southern sea otter, hunted almost to extinction for its fur, now faces threats from oil spills and other sources. If you want to learn more about sea otters and ways you can help save them, send for this education packet and official Friends of the Sea Otter sticker.

Directions:	Write your request on paper, and put it in an envelope. You must enclose a long self-addressed, stamped envelope.
Write to:	Friends of the Sea Otter 140 Franklin Street Suite 309 Monterey, CA 93940
Ask for:	Education packet and sticker

Beavers

Beavers help conserve water and prevent drought and flood. But many beavers are killed for their fur or when their work interferes with that of humans. Now you can help! Read about the Beaver Defenders, a friendly beaver named Chopper, and how you can get involved.

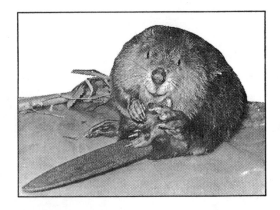

Directions:	Write your request on paper, and put it in an envelope. You must enclose a long self-addressed, stamped envelope.
Write to:	The Beaver Defenders P.O. Box 765 Newfield, NJ 08344
Ask for:	Beaver information

Saving Species

The Nature Conservancy is working hard to protect the world's animal and plant species. One way they do this is by purchasing the deserts, mountains, and wetlands inhabited by our endangered wildlife. One way *you* can help is by learning about conservation and ecosystems from this coloring poster.

Directions: Use a postcard.		
Write to:	The Nature Conservancy Member Relations 1815 North Lynn Street Arlington, VA 22209	
Ask for:	Coloring poster	

FREE

Protection

The Wilderness Society is working to protect America's wilderness and wildlife. They know that protecting the forests, deserts, and wetlands also helps keep the animals who live in these areas safe. Learn more about conserving the wilderness with this fact sheet. You'll also get some wilderness stamps.

Directions:	Write your request on paper, and put it in an envelope. You must enclose a long self-addressed, stamped envelope.
Write to:	The Wilderness Society Membership Services, FSFK 900 17th Street, NW Washington, DC 20006
Ask for:	Fact sheet and wilderness stamps (*Teachers—please order only one packet per classroom.*)

Bluebirds

Our bluebird population has declined rapidly over the last half century, and soon these birds could disappear altogether. If you're concerned about this trend, learn about the North American Bluebird Society. They'll send you an informational pamphlet, directions for building a nesting box, and a sticker with a bluebird on it.

Directions:	Write your request on paper, and put it in an envelope. You must enclose **$1.00.**
Write to:	North American Bluebird Society Department B P.O. Box 6295 Silver Spring, MD 20916-6295
Ask for:	Pamphlet, nesting box plans, and sticker

Sea Turtles

Have a heart for sea turtles! The Kemp's Ridley sea turtles are endangered, and you can help save them from extinction. HEART (Help Endangered Animals—Ridley Turtles) will send you a membership card, turtle surprise gift, and information sheet.

Directions:	Write your request on paper, and put it in an envelope. You must enclose a long self-addressed, stamped envelope and **$1.00.**
Write to:	HEART P.O. Box 681231 Houston, TX 77268-1231
Ask for:	Membership card, gift, and sheet

Marine Magazine

The Cousteau Society cares about all forms of marine life, from whales to starfish. Their magazine, *Dolphin Log,* will help you learn to care, too. Find out about marine animals like the manatee and how people are working to protect them.

Directions:	Write your request on paper, and put it in an envelope. You must enclose **$1.00.**
Write to:	The Cousteau Society 870 Greenbrier Circle, Suite 402 Chesapeake, VA 23320 Attention: Joanne M. Thiele
Ask for:	*Dolphin Log* sample

Marine Life

The Marine Mammal Stranding Center helps save the many sea turtles, seals, dolphins, and whales that are washed ashore along the New Jersey beaches each year. If you care about marine life, send for their bumper sticker that reads "Club Soda—Not Seals!"

Wildlife

The efforts of one man, Brian Davies, helped stop the commercial hunt of baby harp and hood seals. It took over twenty years, but for now they are out of danger. His IFAW (International Fund for Animal Welfare) is still working hard to save animals from cruelty worldwide. Send for their materials to find out more.

Directions:	Write your request on paper, and put it in an envelope. You must enclose a long self-addressed, stamped envelope and **$1.00.**
Write to:	Marine Mammal Stranding Center P.O. Box 773 Brigantine, NJ 08203-0773
Ask for:	Bumper sticker

Directions:	Use a postcard.
Write to:	IFAW P.O. Box 193, Building 2 Yarmouth Port, MA 02675
Ask for:	Fact sheets and animal stickers

Hunting

Some African animals—like rhinos, elephants, and gorillas—are now endangered because of the work of hunters. Learn about these species from the African Wildlife Foundation's information packets for kids. You can also send for a bumper sticker or button that reads "Only Elephants Should Wear Ivory." Specify which items you want.

ONLY ELEPHANTS SHOULD WEAR IVORY
AFRICAN WILDLIFE FOUNDATION

WASHINGTON, D.C. CALL 1-800-344-TUSK OR 202-265-8393   NAIROBI, KENYA CALL 23235

Directions: Use a postcard.

Write to: African Wildlife Foundation
1717 Massachusetts Avenue NW
Suite 602
Washington, DC 20036

Ask for:
- Rhino info
- Elephant info
- Gorilla info
- Button
- Bumper sticker

Endangered Species

Every plant and animal species plays a valuable role in our world. The loss of one species can affect the food chain, medical advancements, agriculture, the environment, and more! This pamphlet further explains why it is important to save endangered species and tells what you can do to help.

Directions: Use a postcard.

Write to: Consumer Information Center
Department 587Z
Pueblo, CO 81009

Ask for: Why Save Endangered Species? pamphlet

Animal Magnets

Discover the many different breeds of cats and dogs with these animal stamp magnets. You can request either a cat or dog magnet—it's a surprise which kind of cat or dog magnet you'll get.

Directions:	Write your request on paper, and put it in an envelope. You must enclose **75¢** for **each** magnet you request.
Write to:	Hicks Specialties Department M4 1308 68th Lane North Brooklyn Center, MN 55430
Ask for:	• Cat magnet • Dog magnet

Kindness

A little bit of kindness can go a long way! Find out about the many steps you can take to save animals by sending for these free materials.

Directions:	Write your request on paper, and put it in an envelope. You must enclose a long self-addressed, stamped envelope.
Write to:	ISAR Department A 421 South State Street Clarks Summit, PA 18411
Ask for:	Free informational materials

Helping Animals

There's a place where animals who are neglected or abused can go for good care—it's called the Popcorn Park Zoo and is part of the Associated Humane Societies. You can learn about this organization and animal care from their reading materials. You may request one or more items.

Needing Animals

The Delta Society believes that animals can improve the lives and well-being of people. They also believe that people can improve animals' lives by being good pet owners. Send for one of their logo decals or their free bibliography on human-animal interactions.

Directions:	Write your request on paper, and put it in an envelope. You must enclose **$1.00.**
Write to:	Associated Humane Societies Department F 124 Evergreen Avenue Newark, NJ 07114
Ask for:	• Wildlife Club booklet • Popcorn Park coloring book • Allergy-Proofing booklet • Humane News booklet

Directions:	Write your request on paper, and put it in an envelope. You must enclose a long self-addressed, stamped envelope for **each** item, plus **$1.00** for **each** logo decal you request.
Write to:	DELTA SOCIETY® P.O. Box 1080 Renton, WA 98057-1080
Ask for:	• Free materials for kids • Decal (*You may choose from the cat, dog, bird, animals, or nature logo.*)

Making Decisions

You might be asked to "dissect" in a science class at school—this means cutting up a dead animal to study it. If you feel sad or uncomfortable about this experience, that's okay. The Animal Legal Defense Fund is behind you and has a handbook that helps explain the issue and alternatives.

Directions:	Use a postcard or call 1-800-922-FROG. (*Include your grade.*)
Write to:	Dissection Hotline Route 1, Box 541 Waynesville, NC 28786
Ask for:	• Saying no to dissection handbook (grades K–6) • Objecting to dissection handbook (grades 7–12)

Spreading the Word

If you don't want to dissect animals, People for the Ethical Treatment of Animals can help. They have some literature, a button, and a bumper sticker you can send for that explains what you can do and what the alternatives are.

Directions:	Use a postcard. (*Include your grade.*)
Write to:	PETA Education Department P.O. Box 42516 Washington, DC 20015-0156
Ask for:	Cut Out Dissection packet

COLLECTIONS
AND HOBBIES

Coin Collecting

Coin collecting is a hobby that's been around since the seventh century B.C. Anyone can start a collection—all it takes is a little know-how. This fifteen-page booklet will tell you how to start a collection and how to preserve your coins once you get them.

Directions:	Write your request on paper, and put it in an envelope. You must enclose a long self-addressed, stamped envelope with **two 29¢** stamps.
Write to:	American Numismatic Association Membership Department—KS 818 North Cascade Avenue Colorado Springs, CO 80903
Ask for:	Coin Collecting booklet

Foreign Money

You can be a numismatist! It's easier than it sounds. All you need is some coins and something to store them in. Here's an assortment of coins from eight different countries to get you started. You can also order some colorful foreign currency. Specify which set you want.

Directions:	Write your request on paper, and put it in an envelope. You must enclose a long self-addressed, stamped envelope, **$1.00**, and **two 29¢** stamps for **each** item you request.
Write to:	Dolphin Point Marketing Department C 32-B Shelter Cove Hilton Head Island, SC 29928
Ask for:	• Foreign coins • Foreign currency

Stamp Collecting

Being a philatelist is fun! The Junior Philatelists of America is a club for kids who like to collect stamps. Send for their multi-page newsletter to learn all the latest information about stamp collecting.

Directions:	Write your request on paper, and put it in an envelope. You must enclose a long self-addressed, stamped envelope and **$1.00.**
Write to:	Junior Philatelists of America P.O. Box 850-P Boalsburg, PA 16827-0850
Ask for:	Newsletter

Stamps

Do you want to start your own stamp collection? Then send for this beginning stamp collector's packet. You'll get information on how to start your collection and a packet of stamps to get you started.

Directions:	Write your request on paper, and put it in an envelope. You must enclose a long self-addressed, stamped envelope.
Write to:	Junior Philatelists of America P.O. Box 850-FS Boalsburg, PA 16827-0850
Ask for:	Beginning stamp collector's packet

Postcards

Have you ever heard of a deltiologist? That's a person who collects postcards. You can start a postcard collection of your own when you send for this beginner's postcard packet. It includes five postcards from different eras and regions, plus some instructions.

Directions:	Write your request on paper, and put it in an envelope. You must enclose a long self-addressed, stamped envelope and **$1.00**.
Write to:	Joan Nykorchuk 13236 North 7th Street, #4 Suite 237 Phoenix, AZ 85022
Ask for:	Beginner's postcard packet

History Postcards

If you've ever read the Little House on the Prairie books or watched the TV show, you probably know that the stories are based on an actual family. These postcards are special because they show true-life photographs of Laura Ingalls and her family. You'll get three.

CARRIE, MARY, LAURA
INGALLS

Directions:	Write your request on paper, and put it in an envelope. You must enclose a long self-addressed, stamped envelope and **$1.00**.
Write to:	Bluestocking Press Department MFSK2 P.O. Box 1014 Placerville, CA 95667
Ask for:	Three Ingalls postcards

Munsters Postcard

Are you a fan of America's funniest family of fright? This collector's postcard features Herman, Lily, Grandpa, Marilyn, and Eddie brewing a secret potion.

Directions:	Write your request on paper, and put it in an envelope. You must enclose a long self-addressed, stamped envelope and **$1.00.**
Write to:	The Munsters Fan Club Department Postcard P.O. Box 69A04 West Hollywood, CA 90069
Ask for:	The Munsters postcard

Addams Family Postcard

They're creepy and they're kooky, mysterious and ooky. They're altogether spooky—The Addams Family! This collector's postcard features Gomez, Morticia, Lurch, Pugsley, and Wednesday gathered around their gold harpsichord.

Directions:	Write your request on paper, and put it in an envelope. You must enclose a long self-addressed, stamped envelope and **$1.00.**
Write to:	The Addams Family Fan Club Department Postcard P.O. Box 69A04 West Hollywood, CA 90069
Ask for:	The Addams Family postcard

Puppets

Collect these fun and realistic paddle puppets! Each puppet mask has a handle and peepholes over the eyes so you can watch your audience react to your play or story. There are 30 puppets in all—everything from a terrifying Tyrannosaurus rex to a cute koala bear.

Directions:	Write your request on paper, and put it in an envelope. You must enclose **$1.25.** (*We think this offer is a good value for the money.*)
Write to:	Spizzirri Publishing Department PP P.O. Box 9397 Rapid City, SD 57709
Ask for:	Paddle puppet (*You may request a dinosaur or an animal.*)

Autographs

If you want to start your own autograph collection, send for this list that features the addresses of famous movie stars, singers, sports figures, astronauts, and politicians. You might get the autograph of someone famous!

Directions:	Write your request on paper, and put it in an envelope. You must enclose a long self-addressed, stamped envelope and **50¢.** (*No checks please.*)
Write to:	Autograph Address List Collector's Club/Department MFSK P.O. Box 467 Rockville Center, NY 11571-0467
Ask for:	Autograph address list

Model Railroads

Building model railroads and trains is lots of fun—especially because you're making something that moves! This colorful, picture-filled booklet will show you what this unique hobby is all about.

Directions:	Use a postcard.
Write to:	Kalmbach Publishing 21207 Crossroads Circle Waukesha, WI 53187 Attention: Marketing/Donations Department
Ask for:	Your Introduction to Model Railroading booklet

Spacemodeling

You can run your own miniature Cape Canaveral. Spacemodeling is the space-age hobby that's great for school projects, science fairs, or just for fun. This pamphlet will tell you more.

Directions:	Use a postcard.
Write to:	National Association of Rocketry P.O. Box 317 Shakopee, MN 55379
Ask for:	Spacemodeling pamphlet

Harmonicas

If you love to play the harmonica (or just love music), send for these fun booklets from Hohner. One booklet teaches you how to play the harmonica, and the other gives fun facts about this instrument.

Directions:	Write your request on paper, and put it in an envelope. You must enclose a long self-addressed, stamped envelope for **each** item you request.
Write to:	Hohner Department MFS94 P.O. Box 9375 Richmond, VA 23227
Ask for:	• How to Play the Harmonica booklet • EasyReeding booklet

Jump-Rope Rhymes

Start skipping! Here's a mini book that fits in your pocket with the words to 29 jump-rope rhymes. You'll find "Fudge, Fudge," "Miss Lucy Had a Baby," "Anna Banana," and more!

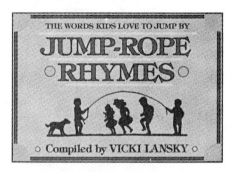

Directions:	Write your request on paper, and put it in an envelope. You must enclose a long self-addressed, stamped envelope and **$1.00.**
Write to:	Practical Parenting Department FS-JR Deephaven, MN 55391-3200
Ask for:	Jump-Rope Rhymes booklet

Chess

Whether you're a beginner at chess or play the game like a pro, take a look at this booklet that features all the moves and rules. You'll soon be saying "Checkmate" with confidence.

Directions:	Write your request on paper, and put it in an envelope. You must enclose a **mailing label** with your return address on it.
Write to:	Dover Publications Department HPC 31 East 2nd Street Mineola, NY 11501
Ask for:	How Do You Play Chess? booklet

Mazes

Are you crazy for mazes? Then send for one of these booklets with 29 different mazes that are fun and challenging.

Directions:	Write your request on paper, and put it in an envelope. You must enclose **$1.25.** (*We think this offer is a good value for the money.*)
Write to:	Spizzirri Publishing Department M P.O. Box 9397 Rapid City, SD 57709
Ask for:	Maze book (*You may request a bird, fish, reptile, animal, plant life, or dinosaur book.*)

Magic Trick

Do you want to amaze your friends and family with a mysterious, magical mind-reading trick? With this set of mind-reading cards, it's easy. You'll also get a fun-filled catalog that contains over 200 tricks and jokes.

Directions:	Write your request on paper, and put it in an envelope. You must enclose **$1.25.** (*We think this offer is a good value for the money.*)
Write to:	Abracadabra Magic and Fun Shop Department C-629 125 Lincoln Boulevard Middlesex, NJ 08846
Ask for:	Mind-reading cards and tricks catalog

Magic Dinosaur

Watch this incredible growing dinosaur get bigger and bigger before your very eyes! All you do is put it in water, and it will grow for up to ten days straight. When you take it out of the water, it will shrink back down to its original size—like magic!

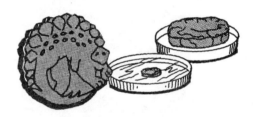

Directions:	Write your request on paper, and put it in an envelope. You must enclose a long self-addressed, stamped envelope and **$1.00.**
Write to:	Neetstuf Department N-124 P.O. Box 459 Stone Harbor, NJ 08247
Ask for:	Dinosaur water creature

CATALOGS

Here are some free catalogs of books, toys, games, music, and more! Just write to the addresses listed below and ask for a "free catalog."

Art supplies
KidsArt
P.O. Box 274
Mount Shasta, CA 96067

Books
John Wiley & Sons, Inc.
605 Third Avenue
New York, NY 10158-0012
Attention: Fred Nachbaur

Meadowbrook Press
Kids' Catalog Department
18318 Minnetonka Boulevard
Deephaven, MN 55391

Games
Aristoplay, LTD
P.O. Box 7529
Ann Arbor, MI 48107

Kites
Into the Wind
1408 Pearl Street
Boulder, CO 80302

Learning materials
Chaselle, Inc.
Marketing Department
9645 Gerwig Lane
Columbia, MD 21046
Request: Book of Early Learning

Consumer Information Catalog
Pueblo, CO 81009

Schneider Educational Products
P.O. Box 472260
San Francisco, CA 94147

Models
Estes Industries
Department 761
1295 H Street
Penrose, CA 81240

Music
A Gentle Wind
Box 3103
Albany, NY 12203

Music for the Little People
P.O. Box 1460
Redway, CA 95560

Toys
The Complete Collegiate/Traveler
P.O. Box 11145
Fairfield, NJ 07004

Expressions
Department FC
1668 Valtec Lane
Boulder, CO 80301

Justa Dollar
17000 Tideview Drive
Anchorage, AK 99516-4833

Videos
Children's Circle
Department MS-C
389 Newtown Turnpike
Weston, CT 06883

FREE

If your family is planning a trip, you'll want to send for these amusement park information packets. Every park listed here will send something special. Just write to the addresses listed below and ask for "free park information."

California
Marine World Africa USA
Travel Marketing Department
Marine World Parkway
Vallejo, CA 94589

Sea World of California
Public Relations Department
1720 South Shores Road
San Diego, CA 92109

Florida
Cypress Gardens
P.O. Box 1
Cypress, FL 33884

Sea World
7007 Sea World Drive
Orlando, FL 32821
Attention: Sales Department

Universal Studios Florida
Information Department
1000 Universal Studios Plaza
Orlando, FL 32819

Indiana
Holiday World
P.O. Box 179
Santa Claus, IN 47579

Redbrush Park
P.O. Box 100
Seymour, IN 47274

Missouri
Worlds of Fun and Oceans of Fun
Public Relations Department
4545 Worlds of Fun Avenue
Kansas City, MO 64161

New Hampshire
Canobie Lake Park
Marketing Department
P.O. Box 190
North Policy Street
Salem, NH 03079

New Jersey
Action Park
P.O Box 848
McAfee, NJ 07428

Ohio
Cedar Point
Marketing Department
P.O. Box 5006
Sandusky, OH 44871-8006

Pennsylvania
Hersheypark
Public Relations Department
100 West Hersheypark Drive
Hershey, PA 17033

Virginia
Paramount's Kings Dominion
P.O. Box 2000
Doswell, VA 23047

Wisconsin
Riverview Park and Water World
P.O. Box 300
Wisconsin Dells, WI 53965
Attention: Craig

U.S. MAIL

MATH, SCIENCE, AND COMPUTERS

Metric System

The United States is the only industrialized country in the world not officially using the metric system. You can learn about the metric system with this booklet. It explains how this ten-unit system works, contains a metric conversion sheet, and even includes a yummy metric chocolate chip cookie recipe.

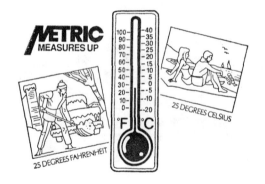

Directions: Use a postcard.

Write to: Consumer Information Center
Department 589Z
Pueblo, CO 81009

Ask for: Metric Measures Up booklet

History Ruler

Now you can learn math and history at the same time. This extra-long ruler with inches and centimeters features pictures of the presidents and the lyrics to the *Star-Spangled Banner*.

Directions: Write your request on paper, and put it in an envelope. You must enclose **$1.00.**

Write to: Smiles 'n Things
P.O. Box 974
Claremont, CA 91711-0974

Ask for: Presidential ruler

Money Quiz

What is money? You may be surprised to find out that a dollar means one ounce of silver. Send for this money trivia quiz to learn more about money, its origins, and why it's valuable.

Directions:	Write your request on paper, and put it in an envelope. You must enclose a long self-addressed, stamped envelope and **50¢.**
Write to:	Money Trivia Bluestocking Press P.O. Box 1014-MFSK2 Placerville, CA 95667
Ask for:	Money Trivia Quiz pamphlet

Money and Banks

You don't have to wait until you go to college to learn about economics. Here are five comic books that will help you understand money, inflation, international trade, and how banks and checks work. Specify which comic books you want.

Directions:	Use a postcard.
Write to:	Federal Reserve Bank of New York Public Information Department 13th Floor 33 Liberty Street New York, NY 10045
Ask for:	• Story of Checks comic book • Too Much, Too Little comic book • Story of Inflation comic book • Story of Foreign Trade comic book • Once Upon a Dime comic book

Coal

Where does coal come from? What is it used for? How does it affect the environment? You can find the answers to these questions and others in these three fact-filled booklets from the American Coal Foundation. Specify which booklets you want.

Directions: Use a postcard.

Write to: American Coal Foundation
1130 17th Street NW, Suite 220
Washington, DC 20036

Ask for:
• Let's Learn about Coal booklet
• Power from Coal booklet
• Electricity from Coal booklet

Cotton

Did you know that the ancient Egyptians made and wore cotton clothing? This valuable textile has been around for centuries and is currently the leading cash crop in the U.S. This booklet will show you where cotton grows and how it is harvested, ginned, and marketed.

Directions: Use a postcard.

Write to: National Cotton Council
Communications Services Department
Box 12285
Memphis, TN 38182

Ask for: The Story of Cotton booklet

Science Experiments

Now, thanks to the "Newton's Apple" TV show and 3M, you can have six science experiments right at your fingertips! With this "Science Try Its"™ sheet you'll be able to do fun and easy science experiments at home. Try to guess what will happen and why, and then compare your results to the answers on the back of the sheet.

Directions:	Write your request on paper, and put it in an envelope. You must enclose a long self-addressed, stamped envelope.
Write to:	Lynae Berge Newton's Apple Science Try Its 172 East Fourth Street, Box 1100 St. Paul, MN 55101
Ask for:	Science Try Its

Science Newsletter

Join the Science for Every Kid Club and receive this informative newsletter. It features science and earthcare information, science activities, word puzzles, and more!

Directions:	Write your request on paper, and put it in an envelope. You must enclose a long self-addressed, stamped envelope.
Write to:	John Wiley & Sons 605 Third Avenue New York, NY 10158 Attention: Fred Nachbaur
Ask for:	Science for Every Kid Newsletter

Conservation

Be an ocean saver! Learn how you can make a difference to the environment. This pamphlet gives tips on what you can do every day to save water, keep the oceans cleaner, and recycle.

CATCH OUR WAVE!

LITTLE HELPERS CAN MAKE
BIG SPLASHES

**I'M AN
OCEAN SAVER**

Practical Suggestions For
Cleaner Oceans

Directions:	Write your request on paper, and put it in an envelope. You must enclose a long self-addressed, stamped envelope.
Write to:	Schneider Educational Products P.O. Box 472260 San Francisco, CA 94147
Ask for:	I'm An Ocean Saver pamphlet

Space Ruler

This ruler is out of this world. It features colorful space holograms—watch the spaceships and astronauts move as you convert from inches to centimeters.

Directions:	Write your request on paper, and put it in an envelope. You must enclose **$1.00.**
Write to:	IPM Department MS-1 P.O. Box 1181 Hammond, IN 46325
Ask for:	Space ruler

Solar System Facts

You can have solar system facts right at your fingertips with this handy chart. Find the average length of a year on Pluto, the temperature on Venus, or the atmosphere on Mars.

Directions: Write your request on paper, and put it in an envelope. You must enclose a long self-addressed, stamped envelope and **10¢.**

Write to: Solar System
Education Department
Hansen Planetarium
15 South State Street
Salt Lake City, UT 84111-1590

Ask for: Solar system fact sheet

Space Cards

Hey, space nuts! Here are some hologram space cards featuring scenes from space. The backs of the cards have interesting facts about space missions, astronauts, and the space program.

Directions: Write your request on paper, and put it in an envelope. You must enclose **$1.00.**

Write to: Joan Nykorchuk
13236 North 7th Street, #4
Suite 237
Phoenix, AZ 85022

Ask for: Four space motion cards

Computer Games

This computer disk is filled with all sorts of fun holiday games and activities for kids. It has dancing bears and elves, a word scramble activity, and a challenging basketball game where you have to sink the ball into a Christmas stocking. (*This 5 ¼-inch disk requires an IBM PC compatible, CGA graphics, and will run on VGA and EGA.*) Try it!

Directions: Write your request on paper, and put it in an envelope. You must enclose a **mailing label** with your return address on it and **$2.00.** (*We think this offer is a good value for the money.*)

Write to: CHEER!
Prentice Associates
4 Maple Street, Suite 2
Quincy, MA 02169

Ask for: CHEER! disk

WRITING SUPPLIES

Design Pencils

Add a splash of color to your desk. These pencils have bright swirly and marble designs. You'll get two.

Directions:	Write your request on paper, and put it in an envelope. You must enclose a long self-addressed, stamped envelope and **$1.00.**
Write to:	Marlene Monroe Department MP 6210 Ridge Manor Drive Memphis, TN 38115-3411
Ask for:	Two swirly/marble pencils

Picture Pencils

Here are some pencils that really make writing fun. They have neat pictures of masks, musical notes, and soccer balls on them. It's a surprise which two you'll get!

Directions:	Write your request on paper, and put it in an envelope. You must enclose a long self-addressed, stamped envelope and **$1.00.**
Write to:	Marlene Monroe Department PP 6210 Ridge Manor Drive Memphis, TN 38115-3411
Ask for:	Two picture pencils

Spooky Pencil

You don't have to wait until Halloween to get one of these ghoulishly great pencils that feature either skeletons and ghosts or bright orange pumpkins. You'll even get a big pumpkin eraser to go on the end of the pencil.

Directions:	Write your request on paper, and put it in an envelope. You must enclose **$1.00.**
Write to:	Smiles 'n Things P.O. Box 974 Claremont, CA 91711-0974
Ask for:	Spooky pencil

Fruity Pencils

These pastel pencils smell super! They're scented in your favorite fruity flavors like lemon, strawberry, orange, apple, and grape. You'll get two.

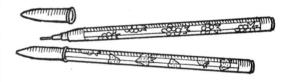

Directions:	Write your request on paper, and put it in an envelope. You must enclose a long self-addressed, stamped envelope and **$1.00.**
Write to:	Maxxine's Fun Toys Department MFS P.O. Box 14415 Philadelphia, PA 19115
Ask for:	Two fruity pencils

Automatic Pencil

Start writing! Here's a pencil that never needs to be sharpened. You'll get one automatic pencil, a twelve-piece tube of refill lead, and an instruction sheet.

Directions: Write your request on paper and put it in an envelope. You must enclose **$1.00.**

Write to: Pentel's Starter Set Offer
2805 Columbia Street
Torrance, CA 90509

Ask for: Automatic pencil set

Make Stationery

Send some really special letters to your friends and family. This kit offers four pieces of stationery that fold over into envelopes, stationery seals, and some rubber bands. Add a spool and ink pad, and you can start making rubber stamp designs for each letter. It's fun and easy!

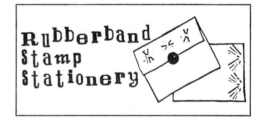

Directions: Write your request on paper, and put it in an envelope. You must enclose **$1.00.**

Write to: Alaska Craft Stationery
Department RSFS
P.O. Box 11-1102
Anchorage, AK 99511-1102

Ask for: Stamp stationery

Sporty Erasers

If you're into sports, try out these fun erasers that are shaped like mini sports balls. You'll get a mini baseball, basketball, and soccer ball eraser.

Bicycle Eraser

This is no ordinary eraser! It's shaped like a bike and has eraser wheels that you can roll right across your desk.

Directions:	Write your request on paper, and put it in an envelope. You must enclose a long self-addressed, stamped envelope and **75¢.**
Write to:	Marlene Monroe Department SE 6210 Ridge Manor Drive Memphis, TN 38115-3411
Ask for:	Sporty erasers

Directions:	Write your request on paper, and put it in an envelope. You must enclose a long self-addressed, stamped envelope and **$1.00.**
Write to:	Marlene Monroe Department BE 6210 Ridge Manor Drive Memphis, TN 38115-3411
Ask for:	Bicycle eraser

Friendship Pen

You've heard of friendship bracelets. Now you can get a friendship pen! This friendship pen kit comes with a pen, embroidery thread, and instructions. Give your best buddy a personalized pen!

Directions:	Write your request on paper, and put it in an envelope. You must enclose **$1.00.**
Write to:	Surprise Gift of the Month Club Department FP P.O. Box 1 Stony Point, NY 10980
Ask for:	Friendship pen

Clown Pen

Are you the class clown? Then send for this clown pen! It's crazy and colorful—plus you can wear it like a necklace so you won't ever lose it.

Directions:	Write your request on paper, and put it in an envelope. You must enclose a long self-addressed, stamped envelope and **$1.00.**
Write to:	The Complete Traveler Department M P.O. Box 11145 Fairfield, NJ 07004
Ask for:	Clown pen/necklace

Alphabet Postcards

These colorful postcards capture the juiciness of an apple, the chill of an ice cube, and the zigzag of a zipper. Each letter is in the form of an object that begins with that letter. There's a piece of "Candy" for C, a "Guppy" for G, a "Pencil" for P, and more! You'll get two postcards.

Directions:	Write your request on paper, and put it in an envelope. You must enclose **$1.00.**
Write to:	A to Z Marketing P.O. Box 22414 Indianapolis, IN 46222
Ask for:	Two alphabet postcards

Funky Postcards

Who says postcards are just for writing messages on? These colorful postcards also function as a pair of crazy-looking sunglasses. You'll get two.

Directions:	Write your request on paper, and put it in an envelope. You must enclose **$1.00.**
Write to:	Surprise Gift of the Month Club Department PC P.O. Box 1 Stony Point, NY 10980
Ask for:	Two sunglasses postcards

Note Cards

Now you can make your own stationery. Using the pin-punch technique, you can create beautiful designs—it's easy! This kit comes with three note cards, three envelopes, nine patterns, a pin, and instructions.

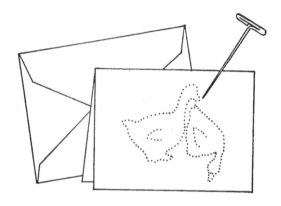

Directions:	Write your request on paper, and put it in an envelope. You must enclose **$1.00.**
Write to:	The Woolie Works—PP 6201 East Huffman Road Anchorage, AK 99516-2440
Ask for:	Pin-punch note kit

Paper and Envelopes

Here's an offer that will please all you letter writers. You can get a set of 20 pieces of writing paper with 15 envelopes or a set of 50 assorted envelopes in great colors and designs. Specify which set you want.

Directions:	Write your request on paper, and put it in an envelope. You must enclose **$1.00** for **each** set you request.
Write to:	Surprise Gift of the Month Club Department S P.O. Box 1 Stony Point, NY 10980
Ask for:	• 20 letters and 15 envelopes • 50 assorted envelopes

MEADOWBROOK PRESS

1994 EDITION

U.S. MAIL

WORLD CULTURES

Native Magazine

Explore the *Daybreak Star*, a 24-page monthly magazine about Native-American peoples and their culture. Each issue contains information about traditional legends and history, current culture and people, plus stories and artwork by student subscribers.

Directions: Write your request on paper, and put it in an envelope. You must enclose a long self-addressed, stamped envelope with **two 29¢** stamps.

Write to: United Indians of All Tribes
1945 Yale Place East
Seattle, WA 98102
Attention: Daybreak Star Reader

Ask for: *Daybreak Star* magazine

Native History

Learn all about the Cherokee Indians—their history, culture, chiefs, and more. These Cherokee National Historical Society materials will help you better understand this fascinating and progressive tribe.

Directions: Use a postcard.

Write to: Cherokee National Historical Society
Education Department—Carol Dunn
P.O. Box 515
Tahlequah, OK 74465

Ask for: Cherokee information

Reading List

Each year the Coretta Scott King Award is given to African-American authors and illustrators whose children's books promote a better understanding of black culture. If you'd like to read some special books by African Americans, send for this pamphlet that lists the award winners and their titles.

CORETTA SCOTT KING AWARD
AND HONOR BOOKS

Directions:	Write your request on paper, and put it in an envelope. You must enclose a long self-addressed, stamped envelope.
Write to:	American Library Association Graphics Department CSK 50 East Huron Street Chicago, IL 60611
Ask for:	Coretta Scott King pamphlet

Newspapers

Harambee is a newspaper for kids that features exciting articles about the African-American experience. You'll find information about black history, culture, and literature plus spotlights on famous African Americans, games and activities, and much more. It's published by Just Us Books—they'll send you their colorful catalog of African American books, too.

"A Newspaper for Young Readers That Focuses on the African-American Experience"

Directions:	Write your request on paper, and put it in an envelope. You must enclose $1.50. *(We think this offer is a good value for the money.)*
Write to:	Just Us Books 301 Main Street, Suite 22-24 Orange, NJ 07050
Ask for:	*Harambee* newspaper and book catalog

Western History

Understanding that our country has always been made up of many different people and races is important to seeing our history as a cultural whole. Here are four postcards that feature historical photographs of African Americans and Native Americans in the nineteenth-century West.

Directions:	Write your request on paper, and put it in an envelope. You must enclose a long self-addressed, stamped envelope for **one** postcard or a long self-addressed, stamped envelope and **$1.00** for **four.**
Write to:	Open Hand Publishing P.O. Box 22048 Seattle, WA 98122
Ask for:	• One free postcard • Four postcards (enclose **$1.00**)

Spanish Language

¿Quieres aprender español? That means "Do you want to learn Spanish?" If you do, send for this free Spanish newsletter that will help you learn the meanings and pronunciations of some Spanish words. It even includes a word game and a special recipe in both Spanish and English.

BUENO

Directions:	Write your request on paper, and put it in an envelope. You must enclose a long self-addressed, stamped envelope.
Write to:	In One EAR Department FS2 29481 Manzanita Drive Campo, CA 91906-1128
Ask for:	Spanish lesson

Jordan

Jordan is a country of great natural beauty, history, and culture. If you're studying the Middle East in Social Studies or Geography and want to learn more, send for this informational material about Jordan—great for school reports!

Austria

Learn all about Austria, Switzerland's neighbor, from these Austrian National Tourist Office materials. You'll find out about Austria's cities, culture, and music, as well as the mighty Austrian Alps.

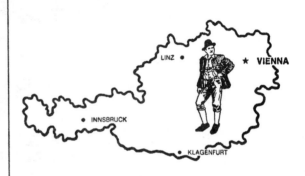

Directions:	Use a postcard.
Write to:	Jordan Information Bureau 2319 Wyoming Avenue NW Washington, DC 20008
Ask for:	Facts and Figures information

Directions:	Use a postcard.
Write to:	Austrian National Tourist Office Kids Department 500 Fifth Avenue New York, NY 10110
Ask for:	Tourist Information Packet

Israel

Israel is one of the world's newest countries, and it has an exciting history and culture. If you want to learn more about it, send for an information packet. (If you have a specific request about Israel's geography, people, or culture that would help you with a school project, indicate this on the postcard.)

The Flag of Israel

Directions:	Use a postcard.
Write to:	The office serving your area (see the next page for a list of all the addresses).
Ask for:	Information packet

If you live in the District of Columbia, Maryland, Virginia, or West Virginia, write to:

Embassy of Israel
3514 International Drive NW
Washington, DC 20008

If you live in Massachusetts, Maine, Vermont, New Hampshire, or Rhode Island, write to:

Consulate General of Israel
1020 Statler Office Building
Boston, MA 02116

If you live in New York, Connecticut, northern New Jersey, Puerto Rico, or the Virgin Islands, write to:

Consulate General of Israel
800 Second Avenue, 15th Floor
New York, NY 10017

If you live in Pennsylvania, Delaware, Ohio, Kentucky, or southern New Jersey, write to:

Consulate General of Israel
230 South 15th Street, 8th Floor
Philadelphia, PA 19102

If you live in Georgia, Alabama, Tennessee, South Carolina, North Carolina, or Mississippi, write to:

Consulate General of Israel
1100 Spring Street, Suite 440
Atlanta, GA 30309

If you live in Illinois, Minnesota, North Dakota, South Dakota, Wisconsin, Indiana, Iowa, Nebraska, Kansas, Michigan, or Missouri, write to:

Consulate General of Israel
111 East Wacker Drive, Suite 1308
Chicago, IL 60601

If you live in Texas, Arkansas, Oklahoma, New Mexico, or Louisiana, write to:

Consulate General of Israel
1 Greenway Plaza East, Suite 722
Houston, TX 77046

If you live in Arizona, southern California, Colorado, Hawaii, Nevada, Utah, or Wyoming, write to:

Consulate General of Israel
6380 Wilshire Boulevard, Suite 1700
Los Angeles, CA 90048

If you live in Alaska, northern California, Oregon, Washington, Montana, or Idaho, write to:

Consulate General of Israel
220 Bush Street, Suite 550
San Francisco, CA 94104

If you live in Florida, write to:

Consulate General of Israel
100 Biscayne Boulevard, Suite 1800
Miami, FL 33132

Send a postcard to the following addresses for tourist information:

Barbados
Barbados Tourism Authority
800 Second Avenue, 17th Floor
New York, NY 10017

Belgium
Belgium National Tourist Office
745 Fifth Avenue, Suite 714
New York, NY 10151

China
China National Tourist Office
60 East 42nd Street, Room 3126
New York, NY 10165

Cyprus
Cyprus Tourist Organization
13 East 40th Street
New York, NY 10016

Denmark
Danish Tourist Board
655 Third Avenue
New York, NY 10017

Finland
Finnish Tourist Board
655 Third Avenue
New York, NY 10017

France
French Government Tourist Office
628 Fifth Avenue
New York, NY 10020

French Government Tourist Office
645 North Michigan Avenue, Suite 630
Chicago, IL 60611-2836

Germany
German National Tourist Office
122 East 42nd Street, 52nd Floor
New York, NY 10168

Greece
Greek National Tourist Organization
645 Fifth Avenue
New York, NY 10022

Greek National Tourist Organization
168 North Michigan Avenue
Chicago, IL 60601

Greek National Tourist Organization
611 West 6th Street, Suite 2198
Los Angeles, CA 90017

Hong Kong
Hong Kong Tourist Association
590 Fifth Avenue
New York, NY 10036

Iceland
Iceland Tourist Board
655 Third Avenue
New York, NY 10017

Ireland
Irish Tourist Board
757 Third Avenue
New York, NY 10017

Italy
Italian Government Travel Office
630 Fifth Avenue
New York, NY 10111

Italian Government Travel Office
500 North Michigan Avenue
Chicago, IL 60611

Japan
Japan National Tourist Organization
401 North Michigan Avenue, Suite 770
Chicago, IL 60611

Kenya
Kenya Tourist Office
424 Madison Avenue
New York, NY 10017

Luxembourg
Luxembourg National Tourist Office
801 Second Avenue
New York, NY 10017

Netherlands
Netherlands Board of Tourism
355 Lexington Avenue, 21st Floor
New York, NY 10017

Netherlands Board of Tourism
225 North Michigan Avenue, Suite 326
Chicago, IL 60601

Netherlands Board of Tourism
90 New Montgomery, Suite 305
San Francisco, CA 94105

Norway
Norwegian Tourist Board
655 Third Avenue
New York, NY 10017

Portugal
Portugese National Tourism Office
590 Fifth Avenue, 4th Floor
New York, NY 10036

St. Lucia
St. Lucia Tourist Board
820 Second Avenue, 9th Floor
New York, NY 10017

Spain
Spanish National Tourist Office
665 Fifth Avenue
New York, NY10022

Spanish National Tourist Office
8383 Wilshire Boulevard, Suite 960
Beverly Hills, CA 90211

Sweden
Swedish Tourist Board
655 Third Avenue
New York, NY 10017

Turkey
Turkish Culture and Tourism Office
1717 Massachusetts Avenue NW, Suite 306
Washington, DC 20036

Note: The Turkish Culture and Tourism Office can provide you with a pen pal. If you would like a pen pal, specify this on your postcard.

Multicultural Magazine

Skipping Stones is a special magazine for kids that celebrates the world's diversity. Inside you'll find lots of stories, poems, international pen pal addresses, photos, and artwork by kids all over the world. Learn about the people of Africa, life in China, the different cultures of South America, and much more.

Directions:	Write your request on paper, and put it in an envelope. You must enclose **$2.00.** (*We think this offer is a good value for the money.*)
Write to:	Skipping Stones Magazine P.O. Box 3939 Eugene, OR 97403-0939
Ask for:	*Skipping Stones* magazine

Foreign Stamp Magnet

Now you can see what stamps from other countries look like! These fun magnets feature colorful foreign stamps. They have your favorite Disney characters on them, too!

Directions:	Write your request on paper, and put it in an envelope. You must enclose **75¢.**
Write to:	Hicks Specialties Department M4 1308 68th Lane North Brooklyn Center, MN 55430
Ask for:	Disney stamp magnet

MEADOWBROOK PRESS
1994 EDITION

U.S. MAIL

AWARENESS AND SELF-ESTEEM

Easter Seals

How should you act when you meet someone with a disability? Find out how people with disabilities feel and how you can be a friend who cares. Send for this pamphlet and bookmark from the Easter Seal Society—it features information and helpful hints.

Directions:	Write your request on paper, and put it in an envelope. You must enclose a long self-addressed, stamped envelope and **$1.00.**
Write to:	More Free Stuff National Easter Seal Society Administrative Services Department 70 East Lake Street Chicago, IL 60601
Ask for:	Easter Seals' stuff

Special Olympics

Special Olympics celebrates the athletic abilities and achievements of people with mental retardation. Their free materials will tell you how this special sports program works and how you can get involved as a volunteer.

Join the World of Winners

Directions:	Use a postcard.
Write to:	Special Olympics International ℅ More Free Stuff for Kids 1350 New York Avenue NW Suite 500 Washington, DC 20005
Ask for:	Free information

Sign Language

Many hearing- and speech-impaired people use sign language to communicate. You can learn the manual alphabet, too. Send for this refrigerator magnet and poster that features the complete manual alphabet. Soon you'll be speaking without making a sound!

Directions:	Write your request on paper, and put it in an envelope. You must enclose a long self-addressed, stamped envelope and **$1.00.**
Write to:	Keep Quiet P.O. Box 361 Stanhope, NJ 07874
Ask for:	Poster and magnet

Stuttering

Stuttering is a speech problem that affects 25 percent of kids at one time or another. You may want to talk for a person who stutters, but you shouldn't. You should try to be patient and take turns talking. Learn more about stuttering in these pamphlets.

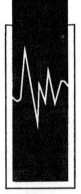

STUTTERING
FOUNDATION
OF AMERICA

Directions:	Use a postcard or call 1-800-992-9392.
Write to:	Stuttering Foundation P.O. Box 11749 Memphis, TN 38111-0749
Ask for:	• If You Think Your Child Is Stuttering pamphlet • The Child Who Stutters at School: Notes to the Teacher pamphlet

Anti-Drug Stickers

Show the world that you don't use drugs! These colorful stickers say "Just Say No to Drugs" and "Drug Free Zone." Put them on your notebooks, locker, or bedroom door. Specify which set you want—you'll get a total of 20 stickers. You may also request a combination of the two types of stickers.

Directions:	Write your request on paper, and put it in an envelope. You must enclose a long self-addressed, stamped envelope and **$1.00** for **each** set you request.
Write to:	Fax Marketing Department M 460 Carrollton Drive Frederick, MD 21701-6357
Ask for:	• Just Say No to Drugs stickers • Drug Free Zone stickers • Combination of stickers

Self-Esteem Stickers

These stickers show that you know you're special. They say things like "I Like Being Me" and "It Feels Good to Be Me." Some even warn you to stay away from drugs. You'll get two sheets.

Directions:	Write your request on paper, and put it in an envelope. You must enclose **$1.00**. *(No checks please.)*
Write to:	Safe Child P.O. Box 40 1594 Brooklyn, NY 11240-1594
Ask for:	Self-esteem stickers

 FREE

Safety Booklet

Operation Lifesaver wants you to stay safe and sound. Their coloring and activity book will show you how to keep out of danger around railroad tracks. You can also get a bookmark that reminds you to "Look, Listen... and Live."

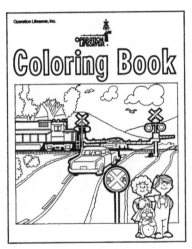

Directions:	Use a postcard.
Write to:	Operation Lifesaver 1420 King Street, Suite 401 Alexandria, VA 22314
Ask for:	• Coloring/activity book • Bookmark (*Limit **one** item per request.*)

Safety Coloring Book

Your body belongs to you and you only. But what if someone tries to touch your body in a way that makes you feel bad? This coloring book will tell you how to deal with that kind of troubling situation.

Directions:	Write your request on paper, and put it in an envelope. You must enclose **$1.00** and **one 29¢** stamp. (*No checks please.*)
Write to:	Safe Child P.O. Box 40 1594 Brooklyn, NY 11240-1594
Ask for:	My Body Belongs to Me coloring book

Being a Teenager

Growing up is serious business, and you might have questions about the changes you're going through. This eight-page booklet for girls, featuring cartoon character Luann, is filled with comic strips and useful information about puberty.

Directions:	Write your request on paper, and put it in an envelope. You must enclose **$1.00.**
Write to:	Girls Incorporated Resource Center Box LU94 441 West Michigan Street Indianapolis, IN 46202
Ask for:	Luann Becomes a Woman booklet

Being a Model

Do you ever wish that you could be a preteen or teen model? This booklet tells you about how this challenging profession can help develop your poise and confidence.

Directions:	Use a postcard. (*Include your age.*)
Write to:	Barbizon Schools Department FK, Suite 300 1900 Glades Road Boca Raton, FL 33431
Ask for:	Free modeling booklet

Girl Scouts Magnet

The Girl Scouts program helps prepare girls to seek and meet the challenges of our ever-changing society. If you're a Girl Scout, or know someone who is, this magnet is a must. It features a U.S. Girl Scouts stamp.

Directions:	Write your request on paper, and put it in an envelope. You must enclose **75¢.**
Write to:	Hicks Specialties Department M4 1308 68th Lane North Brooklyn Center, MN 55430
Ask for:	Girl Scouts magnet

Boy Scouts Magnet

The Boy Scouts of America was founded more than 80 years ago and has been challenging boys to be leaders, provide service to their communities, and have fun ever since. Send for this magnet featuring a U.S. Boy Scouts stamp.

Directions:	Write your request on paper, and put it in an envelope. You must enclose **75¢.**
Write to:	Hicks Specialties Department M4 1308 68th Lane North Brooklyn Center, MN 55430
Ask for:	Boy Scouts magnet

Feeling Special

"You Are Special" is the message of this coloring book. Inside there are lots of activities that will help you learn how to gain self-esteem.

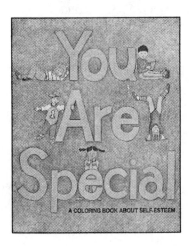

Directions:	Write your request on paper, and put it in an envelope. You must enclose **$1.00** and **one 29¢** stamp. (*No checks please.*)
Write to:	Safe Child P.O. Box 40 1594 Brooklyn, NY 11240-1594
Ask for:	You Are Special coloring book

Having Pride

Whether you're a boy or girl, black or white, or tall or short, you are a special person. This coloring and activity book teaches you about having pride and believing in yourself.

Directions:	Write your request on paper, and put it in an envelope. You must enclose **$1.00** and **one 29¢** stamp. (*No checks please.*)
Write to:	Safe Child P.O. Box 40 1594 Brooklyn, NY 11240-1594
Ask for:	Proud to Be Me coloring book

JEWELRY
AND CRAFTS

Gold Necklace

You can have a heart of gold! This gold necklace with a gold heart charm is fun to wear. You can also request a necklace with a mother-of-pearl heart.

Directions:	Write your request on paper, and put it in an envelope. You must enclose a long self-addressed, stamped envelope and **$1.00** for **each** necklace you request.
Write to:	Mark-It Department 1 P.O. Box 246 Dayton, OH 45405
Ask for:	• Gold heart necklace • Mother-of-pearl heart necklace

Shell Necklace

This necklace is made of beautiful little pieces of colorful shell. It's a perfect gift for someone special.

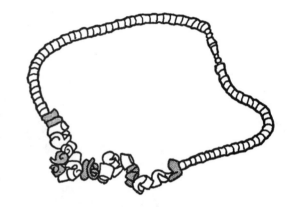

Directions:	Write your request on paper, and put it in an envelope. You must enclose a long self-addressed, stamped envelope and **$1.00**.
Write to:	DANORS Department G 5721 Funston Street, Bay 14 Hollywood, FL 33023
Ask for:	Shell necklace

Whistle Necklace

This colorful necklace is doubly fun! You can whistle your favorite tune with it and wear it around your neck.

Directions: Write your request on paper, and put it in an envelope. You must enclose a long self-addressed, stamped envelope and **$1.00.**

Write to: The Complete Traveler
Department M
P.O. Box 11145
Fairfield, NJ 07024

Ask for: Bear whistle necklace

Best Friend Necklace

Here are two necklaces, one for you and one for your best friend. Each necklace's charm is half of a heart—if you put the charms together you'll have a whole heart that says "Best Friend."

Directions: Write your request on paper, and put it in an envelope. You must enclose **$1.00.**

Write to: Lightning Enterprises
P.O. Box 16121
West Palm Beach, FL 33416

Ask for: Best friend necklace

Friendship Bracelet

This friendship bracelet is really unique—it's made of Ultra-Suede®! The strands are magenta, blue, purple, green, and black. Make the bracelet yourself, using the directions in the kit, and give it to your best friend.

Surfer Bracelets

These surfer bracelets are totally awesome! They come in all sorts of colors and styles—everything from fluorescent to metallic—and it's a surprise which three you'll get. Wear all of them at once for the cool California look.

Directions:	Write your request on paper, and put it in an envelope. You must enclose a self-addressed, stamped envelope and **$1.00.**
Write to:	Pineapple Appeal P.O. Box 197 Owatonna, MN 55060
Ask for:	Ultra-Suede® friendship bracelet kit

Directions:	Write your request on paper, and put it in an envelope. You must enclose **$1.00.**
Write to:	Lightning Enterprises P.O. Box 16121 West Palm Beach, FL 33416
Ask for:	Three surfer bracelets

Colorful Bangles

Send for a bunch of colorful bangles that are shiny and fun to wear! They come in all sorts of colors—when you wear more than one they jangle on your wrist!

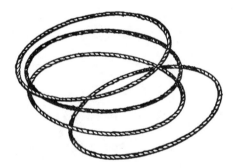

Directions:	Write your request on paper, and put it in an envelope. You must enclose a long self-addressed, stamped envelope and **25¢** for **one** bangle or a long self-addressed, stamped envelope and **75¢** for **four.**
Write to:	Sav-On Department CB P.O. Box 1356 Gwinn, MI 49841
Ask for:	Colorful bangle(s)

Fancy Bracelet

This bracelet has a beautiful mother-of-pearl design. Wear it when you dress up or use it as a gift for your mom, sister, or another special person.

Directions:	Write your request on paper, and put it in an envelope. You must enclose **$1.00.**
Write to:	Sav-On Department FB P.O. Box 1356 Gwinn, MI 49841
Ask for:	Mother-of-pearl bracelet

Art Deco Pins

Here are some fun fluorescent pins that come in shapes and colors galore. You might get a mini piano, a mini Volkswagon, mini sunglasses, or others. Collect a bunch and wear them all on your jean jacket! You'll get two.

Directions:	Write your request on paper, and put it in an envelope. You must enclose a long self-addressed, stamped envelope and **$1.00.**
Write to:	Marlene Monroe Department DP 6210 Ridge Manor Drive Memphis, TN 38115-3411
Ask for:	Art Deco pins (*The supplier reserves the right to choose which two pins you'll get.*)

Personalized Button

Now you can have a cool button featuring your favorite photo! Or you can send a design, quote, stamp, or sticker, and the supplier will create a button for you. (*Just make sure the item you send will fit inside the designed sample below.*)

Directions:	Write your request on paper, and put it in an envelope. You must enclose **$1.00.** (*Include your photo or art.*)
Write to:	Jason Landrigan Department F-2 P.O. Box 82 Diamond Point, NY 12824
Ask for:	Button

Paint Set

Have a heart! This mini paint set comes in a heart-shaped carrying case. It has five colors, a tiny paint brush, and a place to hold the water. It will fit easily into your pocket—paint anywhere!

Directions: Write your request on paper, and put it in an envelope. You must enclose **$1.00.**

Write to: Lightning Enterprises
P.O. Box 16121
West Palm Beach, FL 33416

Ask for: Heart paint set

Fabric Fun

Personalize your clothes, backpack, sneakers, or pillow case. With these pastel dye sticks you can draw a permanent design on a fabric surface. Your design won't wash out or fade! You'll get a set of seven colors and instructions.

Directions: Write your request on paper, and put it in an envelope. You must enclose **$1.00.**

Write to: Pentel's Fabric Fun Offer
2805 Columbia Street
Torrance, CA 90509

Ask for: Fabric fun kit

Scissors

These scissors are perfect for all sorts of arts and crafts projects. They have colorful handles and cut well. Best of all, they fold up so you can store them easily or carry them with you.

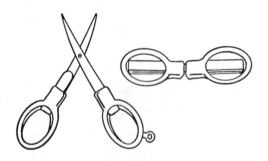

Directions:	Write your request on paper, and put it in an envelope. You must enclose **$1.00.**
Write to:	Eleanor Curran Department S 530 Leonard Street Brooklyn, NY 11222
Ask for:	Folding scissors

Fun Fabric

Have you ever heard of *wearable* art? This apron is made of a special material that you can color, draw, or paint on—create a unique design on it and then wear it to art class or while you're doing arts and crafts projects at home.

Directions:	Write your request on paper, and put it in an envelope. You must enclose a long self-addressed, stamped envelope and **$1.00.**
Write to:	Creative Fun Razers P.O. Box 283 Concord, NC 28026
Ask for:	Child-size apron

Sunglasses Case

This is the coolest case for sunglasses around! It has a bright and colorful design, plus an instruction sheet so you can make it yourself. Use it for your eyeglasses or "shades."

Directions:	Write your request on paper, and put it in an envelope. You must enclose a long self-addressed, stamped envelope and **$1.00.**
Write to:	Pineapple Appeal P.O. Box 197 Owatonna, MN 55060
Ask for:	Sunglasses case kit

Coloring Books

Do you like art and coloring projects? Then **try** these three coloring books about wool growing. They each feature lots of cute sheep and lambs to color. You can order one or all three.

Directions:	Write your request on paper, and put it in an envelope. You must enclose **$1.00** for one coloring book or **$2.00** for **three.** (*We think this offer is a good value for the money.*)
Write to:	Utah Wool Growers 150 South 600 East, Suite 10-B Salt Lake City, UT 84102-1961
Ask for:	• One coloring book (*The supplier reserves the right to choose which one you'll get.*) • Three coloring books

Rubber Stamps

Here are two unmounted rubber stamps that you put together yourself using a spool or old checker and a little rubber cement. There are all sorts of different hobby and animal rubber stamps available—specify your favorites and the supplier will try to provide those for you.

Directions:	Write your request on paper, and put it in an envelope. You must enclose a long self-addressed, stamped envelope with **two 29¢** stamps.
Write to:	RAMASTAMPS Department FSKR 7924 Soper Hill Road Everett, WA 98205
Ask for:	• Two hobby stamps (*Specify your favorites.*) • Two animal stamps (*Specify your favorites.*) • One hobby/One animal stamp (*Specify your favorites.*)

Name Stamp

Personalize all your projects with this cool rubber stamp! Just spell out your first name clearly for the supplier, and you'll soon get a rubber stamp with a wooden handle that has your first name on it.

KELLY

STEPHANIE

Directions:	Write your request on paper, and put it in an envelope. You must enclose **$1.00.**
Write to:	RAMASTAMPS Department FSKR 7924 Soper Hill Road Everett, WA 98205
Ask for:	First name stamp (*Print your first name clearly!*)

INDEX

Activities, 23, 63, 66, 77, 92
Activity books, 32, 89, 92
Aerobics, 24
African Americans, 77–78
Amusement parks, 58
Animals, 24, 38–46, 101–102
Aprons, 100
Archery, 18
Art materials, 57, 99–100
Autographs, 52
Bags, 32
Balloons, 36
Bangles, 97
Baseball, 15, 24, 71
Basketball, 10–15, 24, 66, 71
Beavers, 38
Biking, 24
Birds, 40, 45
Birthdays, 36
Booklets, 13, 17–18, 20, 45, 48, 53–55, 60, 62, 90
Bookmarks, 86, 89
Books, 57
Boomerangs, 16
Bowling, 15, 24
Bracelets, 96–97
Brochures, 10
Bumper stickers, 10–11, 42–43, 46
Buttons, 30, 43, 46, 98
Canoeing, 17

Cards
basketball, 14
football, 14
magic, 56
membership, 16
space, 65
Cartoon characters, 24, 36, 90
Catalogs, 56–57, 77
Cats, 33, 44–45
Chanukah, 34
Charts, 65
Chess, 55
Christmas, 25, 35
Clowns, 26, 72
Clubs, 49, 63
Coal, 62
Coins, 48
Collections, 48–58
Coloring books, 32, 45, 89, 92, 101
Coloring poster, 39
Comic books, 61
Computers, 24, 66
Conservation, 39, 64
Cotton, 62
Crafts, 101–102
Creatures, 26, 56
Cultures, 76–84
Decals, 45
Dinosaurs, 56
Disabilities, 86–87

Dissection, 46
Dogs, 44–45
Drug awareness, 88
Easter, 29
Economics, 61
Endangered species, 41–43
Envelopes, 70, 74
Erasers, 28–29, 69, 71
Experiments, 63
Fan packs, 10–11
Father's Day, 30
Fishing, 24
Fitness, 20
Flags, 31
Footbag, 16
Football, 14–15, 24
Foreign countries, 79–83
Foreign languages, 78
Games, 13, 55, 57, 66, 77
Golf, 24
Hacky Sack, 16
Halloween, 25, 32–33, 69
Handbooks, 46
Harmonicas, 54
Hearts, 28, 95, 99
Hiking, 19
History, 13, 36, 50, 60, 76–78
Hobbies, 48–49, 53, 102
Holidays, 25, 28–36, 66
Holograms, 64–65

INDEX

Horseshoes, 18
Independence Day, 31
Industry, 62
Jack-o'-lanterns, 33, 69
Jewelry, 94–98
Jokes, 56
Jump rope, 54
Key chains, 30
Kites, 57
Kits, 35, 72, 96, 99, 101
Lists, 52, 77
Literature, 77
Magazines, 16, 41, 76, 84
Magic, 56
Magnets, 44, 84, 87, 91
Marine life, 41–42
Math, 60
Mazes, 32, 55
Memo pads, 28
Metric system, 60
Modeling, 90
Models, 53, 57
Money, 61
Monsters, 26
Mother's Day, 30
Music, 54, 57
Native Americans, 76, 78
Necklaces, 72, 94–95
Newsletters, 49, 63, 78
Newspapers, 77

Ornaments, 35
Otters, 38
Packets
    information, 38, 43, 58,
    79–83
    postcard, 50
    stamp, 49
Paint sets, 99
Pamphlets, 12, 17–19, 40, 43,
53, 64, 77, 86–87
Pen pals, 83–84
Pencils, 31, 68, 70
Pens, 72
Pets, 45
Photos, 11
Pins, 98
Pool, 17
Postcards, 50–51, 73, 78
Posters, 39, 87
Puberty, 90
Puppets, 52
Puzzles, 32
Quizzes, 61
Reading lists, 77
Recreation, 16–19
Rhymes, 54
Rubber stamps, 102
Rulers, 60, 64
Safety, 19, 32, 89
Schedules, 10–11
Science, 63–65

Scissors, 100
Sea turtles, 41
Seals, 42
Sheets
    fact, 36, 40, 42, 65
    information, 41
    instructional, 16, 63, 101
    sticker, 15, 22–26, 29, 34, 88
    trick, 19
Sign language, 87
Soccer, 15, 24, 71
Space, 64–65
Spanish, 78
Special Olympics, 86
Sports, 10–20, 24, 71
Stamps, 40, 49, 84, 91
Stationery, 70, 74
Stencils, 33
Stickers, 10–11, 15, 22–26, 29,
31, 34, 38, 40, 42–43, 46, 88
Stuttering, 87
Tape measures, 20, 30
Tennis, 15, 24
Toys, 57
Valentine's Day, 28
Videos, 57
Whistles, 95
Wildlife, 38–40, 42
Wreaths, 35
Writing supplies, 68–74
Yo-Yos, 19

More Books Kids Will Love!

Free Stuff for Kids

By the Free Stuff Editors

If you loved *More Free Stuff for Kids,* be sure to get a copy
of the 1994 edition of the best-selling *Free Stuff for Kids.* It
contains even more of the free stuff you love, including
baseball and hockey fan packs, environmental offers, games,
magazines, posters, coloring books, and more.

Order #2190 $5.00

Kids Pick the Funniest Poems

Compiled by Bruce Lansky
Illustrated by Stephen Carpenter

Three hundred kids can't be wrong—this is one funny book! It
contains the funniest poems for kids because *kids* picked them.
Inside you'll find hilarious poems by Shel Silverstein, Jack Prelutsky,
Jeff Moss, Dr. Seuss, and Judith Viorst, plus lots of poems by new
writers that are just as funny. This book is guaranteed to please kids
ages 6–12.

Order #2410 $14.00 (Hardcover with dust jacket)

The New Adventures of Mother Goose

Created by Bruce Lansky
Illustrated by Stephen Carpenter

Finally—a sequel to the children's classic that is kinder, gentler,
and funnier than the original. It contains all-new rhymes featuring
favorites like Humpty Dumpty and Little Miss Muffet in their new
adventures.

Order #2420 $15.00 (Hardcover with dust jacket)

Order Form

Quantity	Title	Author	Order No.	Unit Cost	Total
	Almost Grown-Up	Patterson, Claire	2290	$5.00	
	Dads Say the Dumbest Things!	Lansky/Jones	4220	$6.00	
	Dino Dots	Dixon, Dougal	2250	$4.95	
	Free Stuff for Kids	Free Stuff Editors	2190	$5.00	
	Grandma Knows Best, But No One Ever Listens!	McBride, Mary	4009	$6.00	
	Hocus Pocus Stir & Cook, Kitchen Science	Lewis, James	2380	$7.00	
	How To Embarrass Your Kids	Holleman/Sherins	4005	$6.00	
	Kids Pick the Funniest Poems	Lansky, Bruce	2410	$14.00	
	Learn While You Scrub, Science in the Tub	Lewis, James	2350	$7.00	
	Measure Pour & Mix, Kitchen Science Tricks	Lewis, James	2370	$7.00	
	Moms Say the Funniest Things!	Lansky, Bruce	4280	$6.00	
	More Free Stuff for Kids	Free Stuff Editors	2191	$5.00	
	Rub-a-Dub-Dub, Science in the Tub	Lewis, James	2270	$6.00	
	Webster's Dictionary Game	Webster, Wilbur	6030	$5.95	
	Weird Wonders and Bizarre Blunders	Schreiber, Brad	4120	$4.95	
	"I Embarrass My Kids Without Even Trying!" Button		4006	$1.00	
				Subtotal	
			Shipping and Handling (see below)		
			MN residents add 6.5% sales tax		
				Total	

YES, please send me the books indicated above. Add $2.00 shipping and handling for the first book and $.50 for each additional book (no additional charges, however, for button orders). Add $2.50 to total for books shipped to Canada. Overseas postage will be billed. Allow up to 4 weeks for delivery. Send check or money order payable to Meadowbrook Press. No cash or C.O.D.'s, please. Prices subject to change without notice. **Quantity discounts available upon request.**

Send book(s) to:

Name _____ Phone _____

Address _____

City _____ State _____ Zip_____

Payment via:

❑ Check or money order payable to Meadowbrook Press. (No cash or C.O.D.'s, please.) Amount enclosed $ _____

❑ Visa (for orders over $10.00 only)   ❑ MasterCard (for orders over $10.00 only)

Account # _____ Signature _____ Exp. Date _____

A *FREE* Meadowbrook Press catalog is available upon request.
You can also phone us for orders of $10.00 or more at 1-800-338-2232.
Mail to: Meadowbrook, Inc., 18318 Minnetonka Blvd., Deephaven, MN 55391
Toll-Free 1-800-338-2232

(612) 473-5400   FAX (612) 475-0736